Living in a Vi

by Jenny Alexand

Contents

Longman

Edinburgh Gate
Harlow, Essex

Paul, Anton, David and Donna

Paul, Anton, David and Donna live in a small village in Devon. The village has its own school because it's a long way from any other villages or towns. There are 23 children in the school. They are split into two classes – infants and juniors. Paul, Anton, David and Donna are the only Year Fours.

Here is what they have to say about growing up in a village.

Paul

I love football but we haven't got enough juniors in our school to get a decent game. There aren't any **Premiership** teams near here. I support Leeds United, but I've only seen them play twice. I've got a friend who lives in Leeds, and he sees nearly every match.

He's got a cinema nearby, a sports hall, a swimming pool and lots of great shops. I think it would be much better living in a town.

Anton

I was born in London. Before we came here I thought it was going to be like the Famous Five, with lots of messing around in the countryside. But you have to stay on the footpaths round here.

I still like it though. My best friend, David, lives on a farm. We have a great time playing in the barns and fields. He's got a huge concrete yard for BMX and skateboarding, too.

David

I live on a farm. My father and grandfather both grew up on the same farm. One day it will belong to me. I get up early to feed the animals before school. At weekends I help with other jobs.

I've got seven cousins at school! I've known everyone in my class since we were at playgroup. That's nice in a way, but not very exciting. So it was great when Anton came.

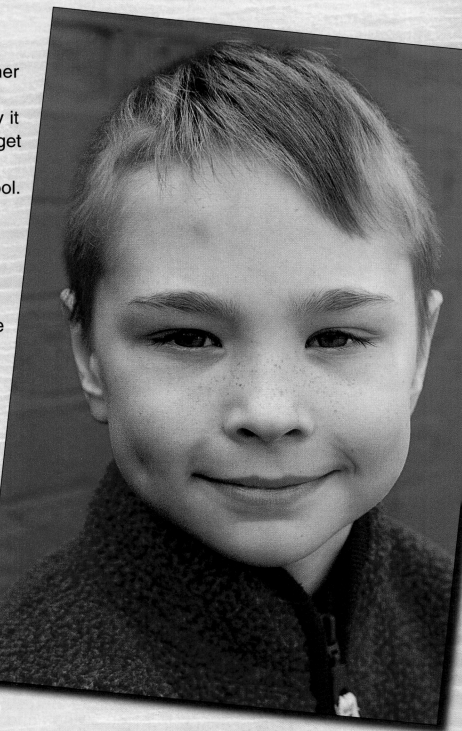

Donna

I quite like living in the village, but I wish there was another girl in my year. I've got friends, but they are older or younger than me.

We've got a playing field with some swings and a climbing frame. We hang around there a lot. The village isn't on a main road, so we can cycle everywhere. On Saturdays, I go horse riding. It's brilliant!

It's Not Like the Old Days!

mill

forge

bakery

My name is Sid Green. I've lived in the same village all my life. I was born in this house. My father was a farm worker. All these cottages used to be for farm workers. These days the farmer doesn't need so many workers because machines can do the work. The house I was born in has become a holiday cottage.

When I was a boy, people didn't have cars, so everyone worked in the village. We had three working farms which sold eggs and vegetables. There was a **forge**, a mill and a bakery. They've all been turned into houses now.

church

artist's studio

The church was the centre of village life. Everyone went to church on Sundays. Not many people go to church any more. We have to share a vicar with two other villages. The **vicarage** has been turned into an artist's studio.

new houses

new school

old school

There are lots of new houses in the village. You can tell by the road names what used to be there before. We've got Old Orchard Close, The Meadows and Cricket Park. More people can live here now because they can drive to work in nearby towns.

The old school was very small. Now there are more children in the village, so we've got a big new school. The old one has been turned into a house.

function room

garden

The Queen's Head

car park

pub

The pub used to be small, too. It had just a bar and a few tables. Now it's got a **function room**, a garden and a big car park, because people come from all around, not just from the village.

We still have a shop in the village, but most people get their shopping once a week in the supermarket in town. There used to be a village post office, too. Now it's just a counter at the back of the shop.

General Stores

post office

sheltered houses

In the old days, a chap my age would have lived with his family. Now we've got these sheltered houses. I can live here safely on my own because there's a warden to look out for me – in case I'm ill or have an accident. I don't have to depend on my family. I like being independent.

Incomers

Incomers are people who come to live in a village from somewhere else. In the past, people didn't move around very much. They tended to spend their whole lives in the place they were born. These days, incomers are a common feature of village life.

Why do people move from towns to villages?

There are lots of reasons why people might choose to move from towns to villages. They include:

a pleasant environment

better air quality

lower house prices

a slower pace of life

a sense of community

less crime

What makes it possible?

The two most important things that make it possible for more people to live in villages are:

1. Cars

Cars mean people can live a long way away from where they work. They can also drive to shops, cinemas and other **amenities** that are mostly found in towns.

Having a car means older people can retire to the country without getting cut off from their family and friends.

2. Communications

Telephones, fax machines, the postal service, computers and the Internet mean more people can work from home – at least for part of the week.

What are the problems?

Sometimes "them and us" feelings can arise. Local people can feel their old way of life is under threat, particularly if too many new people arrive at once. They can resent outsiders buying houses because this makes houses in the village more expensive. When house prices go up, it's hard for young local people to afford to buy a home.

Incomers can feel unwelcome. They may find it difficult to adjust to a different way of living, and have problems becoming part of the village community.

What are the advantages?

Just as it is easier for people to move into villages from towns, it is also easier for people to move out. A lot of young people go away to college and don't come back. Others move to cities to get a better choice of jobs, or because they just prefer the city way of life. In rural areas where there are no incomers, houses fall empty. Then shops, schools and other amenities can be lost.

Incomers bring new skills and ideas into a community. People who have lived in the same place all their lives bring stability. Where local people and incomers respect and value each other, a village can develop and thrive.

Shopping

A village shop and post office

Villages used to be self-contained, with enough shops to provide most of the villagers' needs. Now people have more choices about how and where they shop. Few villages can support more than one shop, and many don't have any shops at all.

Food shopping

A lot of people who live in villages drive to the nearest supermarket once a week to do their food shopping. They don't have to shop locally every day any more because they have fridges and freezers to keep food fresh. Many supermarkets offer a free delivery service, so even people without cars can buy their food from a supermarket. They simply place their order on-line or by phone, and have their food delivered to the door.

Most village shops can't compete with supermarkets. They only stock a limited range of essential foods that people might run out of, like sugar and milk. They have become more like convenience stores, selling less food and more things like videos, newspapers and birthday cards.

Many villages also have mobile shops – vans which come round selling fresh foods like fish, meat, vegetables and bread. Some also still have milk delivered to the door. Although their prices are more expensive, these mobile shops can compete because they save people money on petrol and parking.

Non-food shopping

A lot of villages have no bus services or trains, and it can be difficult for people to get to towns and cities. For people without cars, it can be almost impossible.

So people in rural areas often use **catalogues** for non-food shopping like clothes and gifts. They can place an order by phone and have the goods delivered the next day. They use book clubs and music clubs, which offer books and CDs through the post.

The Internet has been an exciting development for people who live in villages. Internet shopping is giving them the same range of choices and prices as city-dwellers. As well as special on-line shops, most major high street stores also offer on-line shopping.

It may be that country dwellers are leading the way in this shopping revolution. People in towns, who can get to shopping centres relatively easily, may take longer to realise that it's even easier to shop from home.

All Villages Are Different

Villages come in all different shapes and sizes, and what it's like to live in them depends on several factors.

1. Size

Some villages are very compact, with all the houses fairly close together. Others are more spread out, with farms and houses scattered over a wide area.

Some villages have fewer than 100 **inhabitants**. Others can have over 1000. But this doesn't mean they necessarily have more amenities. That can depend more on how remote they are.

2. Remoteness

Villages that are a long way from a town often have more amenities than others that are nearer. This is because it's more difficult for people to go outside the village for shopping and leisure activities. More remote villages will often keep their school, even if it's very tiny; villages close to other **settlements** are more likely to have their small schools closed down.

In remote areas, like the North of Scotland, village shops carry a much wider stock, selling everything from sewing needles to Wellington boots, as well as all the basic foodstuffs.

More remote villages are often served by visiting doctors' surgeries, **mobile libraries** and banks.

3. Transport

What makes a village more or less remote these days is more a question of time than distance. What matters is not so much how far it is to the nearest town, but how long it takes to get there. Villages situated on or near main roads tend to feel less isolated. They are less likely to get cut off by snow in the winter. On the down side, they can also lose some of the quiet charm of villages that are off the beaten track.

4. The surrounding countryside

Some people imagine that living in a village means you can get out into the countryside more easily. In upland areas, or less populated areas, people do have good access to the countryside. But in areas that are more intensively farmed, they have to stick to public footpaths, which may be few and far between.

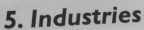

5. Industries

Some villages have grown up around a local industry, like coal mining or farming. These industries used to provide work for the whole community. They also provided a sense of identity. Now people in them are having to find new industries like tourism, because the traditional industries are in decline. Sometimes they can use their history to create tourist attractions, like the Big Pit in Wales.

Visit Wales' National Collections for FREE!

BIG PIT NATIONAL MINING MUSEUM OF WALES
2002

NATIONAL MUSEUMS & GALLERIES OF WALES

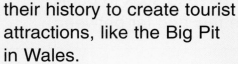

The Most Important Thing

The most important thing for any village is the people who live in it, because everything in a village is run by local people for local people. The Parish Council is a group of people who are elected to serve the local community. They check **planning applications** to make sure that any new buildings blend in with the local style of architecture, and to limit the number of new houses that are built.

Parish councillors try to sort out problems and complaints. For example, they will remind householders that their hedges need cutting back if cyclists and pedestrians complain. They impose and enforce **by-laws** about things like dog fouling and littering.

Village shopkeepers can play a very active part in village life. They usually know everyone, and can tell visitors how to find the place or person they are looking for. They are a great source of information.

Most villages have a public hall. A committee of local people will look after its upkeep and organise lettings. Some of the things that could be offered at the hall include:

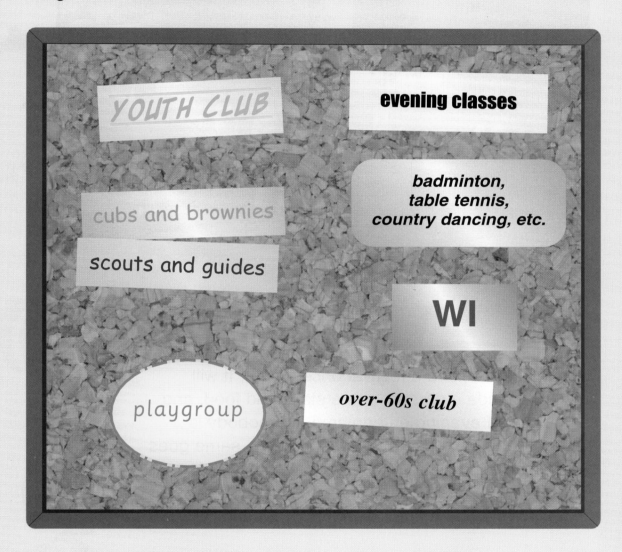

But nothing will be on offer at all in a village hall unless someone volunteers to run it.

Some villages have a festival once a year. It will usually include a parade, some stalls and food, and some sort of evening entertainment. If nobody is willing to organise it, it won't happen. The same goes for **produce shows**. Some villages win prizes for Tidiest Village, Best Floral Displays, and so on, and that also requires a lot of work by local people.

In a village, it isn't only the people who organise things that matter – everyone does. Local clubs can only thrive if people use them and enjoy them. By-laws can only work if most people obey them. Creating a clean and attractive environment depends on everybody helping to keep it that way.

In fact, people are the most important thing in any community – town, city, country, world – it's just that it's more obvious in a village.

Glossary

amenities — pleasant or useful features of a place

by-laws — local rules

catalogues — magazines listing things for sale

forge — blacksmith's workshop, where iron is melted down and hammered out to make things like horseshoes

function room — large room used for dances, discos, parties and meetings

inhabitants — people who live in a particular place

mobile library — walk-in van which contains a selection of books from the public library

planning application — a request to the local authority for permission to build something or alter an existing building

Premiership — the top 20 football clubs in England

produce show — a local competition to see who has grown the best fruit, flowers and vegetables and made the best cakes, wines and jams

settlements — groups of buildings, villages, towns and cities

vicarage — a house owned by the Church for a vicar to live in

WI — Women's Institute – a network of social clubs for women throughout Britain, Canada and the Commonwealth